Shooting Hedda Gabler

Nina Segal, after Henrik Ibsen

methuen | drama

LONDON • NEW YORK • OXFORD • NEW DELHI • SYDNEY

METHUEN DRAMA
Bloomsbury Publishing Plc
50 Bedford Square, London, WC1B 3DP, UK
1385 Broadway, New York, NY 10018, USA
29 Earlsfort Terrace, Dublin 2, Ireland

BLOOMSBURY, METHUEN DRAMA and the Methuen
Drama logo are trademarks of Bloomsbury Publishing Plc

First published in Great Britain 2023

Cover design by Jenny Nicholas

Artwork photography by Michael Wharley

A catalogue record for this book is available from the British Library.

A catalog record for this book is available from the Library of Congress.

ISBN: PB: 978-1-3504-5396-8
ePDF: 978-1-3504-5397-5
eBook: 978-1-3504-5398-2

Series: Modern Plays

Typeset by Mark Heslington Ltd, Scarborough, North Yorkshire

To find out more about our authors and books visit
www.bloomsbury.com and sign up for our newsletters.

**A Rose Original Production in association
with The Norwegian Ibsen Company**

SHOOTING HEDDA GABLER

**By Nina Segal, After Henrik Ibsen
Directed by Jeff James**

*Supported by the Norwegian Embassy, and Cockayne Grants
for the Arts, a donor advised fund held at
The London Community Foundation*

This play was first performed at Rose Theatre
on 29 September 2023 with the following cast:

CAST

Antonia Thomas – Hedda
Christian Rubeck – Henrik
Avi Nash – Ejlert
Anna Andresen – Berta
Matilda Bailes – Thea
Joshua James – Jørgen

CREATIVE

Writer – Nina Segal
Director – Jeff James
Set Designer – Rosanna Vize
Costume Designer – Milla Clarke
Lighting Designer – Hansjörg Schmidt
Composer & Sound Designer – Kieran Lucas
Intimacy & Movement Director – Ingrid Mackinnon
Casting Director – Sam Jones CDG
Voice & Dialect Coach – Anne Whitaker
Assistant Director – Amy Crighton
Assistant Lighting Designer – Emma Gasson

PRODUCTION

Production Manager – Phil Connolly
Costume Supervisor – Hazel McIntosh
Company Stage Manager – Katie Bachtler

Deputy Stage Manager – Katie Bingham
Assistant Stage Manager – Emma Currie
Wardrobe Manager – Lucie Smith
Production Sound Engineer – Kiel Deakin
Sound #1 – Amber Carey
Prod LX – Emma Sayers
LX Programmer – Kat Wellman
Production Carpenter – Toby Lindley
Set Build – Liverpool Scenic Workshops

Commissioned and produced by Rose Theatre (Chief Executive Robert O'Dowd, Artistic Director Christopher Haydon, Executive Producer David Sloan), produced in association with The Norwegian Ibsen Company (Artistic Director Kåre Conradi, Executive Producer André Moi Danielsen)

Shooting Hedda Gabler

For Jeff

Characters

Hedda, *American, actor*
Jorgen, *Norwegian, actor*
Thea, *Norwegian, actor*
Ejlert, *American, actor*
Henrik, *Norwegian, director*
Berta, *Norwegian, first assistant director*

Text intended to be spoken in Norwegian is indicated in *italics* and indented.

Act One

One

Berta *is alone on set.* **Jorgen** *enters.* **Berta** *crosses to him – they hug.*

Berta   Hi –

    Jorgen   *Hey – good to see you –*

Berta   Good to see you too –

    Jorgen   *I can't believe we both came back –*

Berta   English, remember –

    Jorgen   *After last time –*

Berta   Please – in English.

    Jorgen   *You don't speak Norwegian?*

Berta   English.

Jorgen   You don't speak Norwegian?

Berta   Yes – I do –

Jorgen   Our starlet doesn't speak Norwegian –

Berta   No – so, English please. For her. So – you came back?

Jorgen   Glutton for punishment – and you?

Berta   I have a child to feed.

Jorgen   He's in already? Henrik?

Berta   Yes –

Jorgen   The others?

Berta   You're the first.

Jorgen   So maybe I should leave again –

Berta   The call's for ten –

Jorgen   I know –

Berta   It's ten.

Jorgen   I know. So here I am – obedient. While everybody else declares their power through their lateness –

Berta   Being late isn't a power move – it's rude –

Jorgen   And rudeness is a power move.

Hedda *enters.* **Berta** *turns – but* **Jorgen** *is slower to acknowledge her.*

Hedda   Hey –

Berta   Hi –

>   **Jorgen**   *Nice to meet you – I think I recognise you from the television.*

Berta   English –

Jorgen   Nice to meet you –

Hedda   It's – wonderful – to meet you. I've seen all your work –

Jorgen   You have?

Hedda   I mean – I haven't, no. But I've seen – some. And it's – so brilliant. You're a – of our generation – really –

Jorgen   Really?

Hedda   And – being here! In Norway! An incredible country –

Berta   Have you seen much of the country?

Hedda   Only from the window of the car –

Jorgen   They ordered you a car?

Hedda   And – full disclosure – I was asleep for some of it. Or – all of it. The flight – even in business class, it's basically inhumane –

Jorgen   They flew you business class?

Hedda   Of course. That's standard, isn't it?

Berta   Standard class is standard, usually.

Hedda   We haven't met –

Berta   I work for the production –

Hedda   Hair and make-up?

Berta   First AD.

Hedda   Of course. I only thought, because your hair is – is that natural? You'll have to let me know your – really – because that is –

Berta *touches her hair self-consciously.* **Hedda** *turns away, distracted.*

Hedda   Is he here? Henrik?

Berta   He is on set.

Hedda   I'd love to have some time – just he and I –

Berta   I'm sure he'll join us soon –

Hedda   I couldn't just – I'm sure he wouldn't mind –

Berta   I've worked with him before –

Hedda   I haven't. So – I'd like to speak with him.

Berta   I'll ask him –

Hedda   Now?

Tension – then **Berta** *relents.* **Hedda** *smiles. As* **Berta** *starts to exit:*

Hedda   Thank you. And – my bags? They're in the car. Is there a – somebody –

Berta   It is a small crew here. There is no somebody.

Hedda   Of course. So – would you –

Jorgen   I'll get your bags. My job here is to be your husband, after all.

Berta *and* **Jorgen** *exit –* **Hedda** *is alone. She shuts her eyes, attempts to slow her breathing.* **Thea** *enters.* **Hedda** *opens her eyes – and jumps.*

Hedda   Oh fuck –

Thea   I didn't mean to scare you.

Hedda   No, you didn't – I just – didn't expect –

Thea   I work here too. You're not the only one.

Hedda   An actor?

Thea   Yes – how can you tell?

Hedda   You're pretty –

Thea   I like to think that's not why I was cast.

Hedda   Oh no – of course not. But it's part of the equation, isn't it –

Thea   For you, perhaps –

Hedda   For all of us –

Thea   You think you get your work because of men's desire for you?

Hedda   Maybe. And I don't think that's right, but it's the game we play.

Thea   I thought you started working by the age of six –

Hedda   I did –

Thea   And did they cast you then, because of men's desire for you?

Hedda   I was – a child –

Thea   As you say – that's the game we play.

Hedda *is flustered, momentarily – then regains composure.*

Hedda   First job?

Thea   I graduated in the spring – from the academy.

Hedda   The academy? That's – impressive. I am – so impressed. Although it's no match, is it, for experience? For working?

Thea   I am here to work.

Hedda *laughs.* **Thea** *remains straight-faced.*

Thea   That's funny?

Hedda   No. It's just so – serious. Severe –

Thea   I don't think I'm severe.

Hedda   When I was your age –

Thea   You were comatose at an awards ceremony.

Hedda   At least I was at an awards ceremony.

Jorgen *enters, laden down with* **Hedda's** *bags.*

Jorgen   So many bags – it's like you're moving here –

Thea *crosses to* **Jorgen**, *embracing him.*

Thea   How are you? How's the family?

Jorgen   They love me – it's exhausting.

Hedda   You two have met before?

Thea   Through Henrik, yes –

Hedda   You've worked with Henrik then?

Thea   A short film, a few years ago – a small role, but he appreciated my technique and recommended me to the academy –

Hedda   A few years back? So you were –

Thea   Seventeen –

Hedda   And he appreciated your technique, did he? At seventeen?

Berta *enters –* **Thea** *crosses to her. They embrace.*

Berta   Hi – welcome back –

Thea   It's good to be here –

Berta   He's asked to see you – I can take you now –

Hedda   I asked to see him –

Berta   And he asked to see her. So –

Berta *and* **Thea** *turn to exit. To* **Thea***:*

Berta   I'll take you to your trailer on the way –

Hedda   And who will take me to my trailer?

Berta   I'll show her first, then she can show you where it is –

Hedda   But I don't –

Before **Hedda** *can finish her sentence,* **Berta** *and* **Thea** *exit.*

Hedda   I don't share a trailer.

Jorgen   Here, I think you do.

Hedda   I have to call my agent –

Jorgen   So – call your agent.

Hedda *takes out her phone and calls her agent. There is no answer.*

Jorgen   They're not answering your call –

Hedda   They're – busy –

Jorgen   Busy not answering your call. My agent is the same – I thought the problem was my phone – I even bought a new phone, but –

Hedda   We aren't the same –

Jorgen   No. I'm a – of our generation – really –

Hedda *stares at* **Jorgen** – *then laughs. He takes out a pack of cigarettes.*

Jorgen   You want one?

Hedda   I'm trying to quit –

Jorgen   And – do you want one?

Hedda   Of course I do –

Jorgen *offers* **Hedda** *a cigarette. She takes it – but then hands it back.*

Hedda   But – I'm trying to quit.

Jorgen   So – you came to Europe to quit smoking?

Hedda   Something like that –

Jorgen   Because I heard you came here to escape the tabloids, after running down the paparazzi in a self-driving Tesla.

Hedda   It wasn't self-driving – that was the problem.

Jorgen   But the rest is true?

Hedda   You shouldn't believe what you read in gossip magazines.

Jorgen   So you're not a narcissistic ex-teen actor, aged out of your prime and into alcohol dependency and prescription pills?

Hedda   One of those things is true – two, maybe.

Jorgen   I hope it's the alcohol dependency – I could do with company.

Hedda   I don't drink –

Jorgen   That's not what I read in my gossip magazines.

Hedda   Can we talk about something else? Someone else?

Jorgen   Of course – who?

Hedda   Henrik – what's he like?

Jorgen   He's a director. You know what they are like – you dated one –

Hedda   You must read a lot of magazines –

Jorgen   What happened?

Hedda   Just – what happens. It – ended. Not well.

Jorgen   But you didn't crash your Tesla into him?

Jorgen *smiles –* **Hedda** *does not.*

Jorgen   You are upset with me – that's good. We play a married couple – so a little tension will be good. It's realistic –

Hedda   I wouldn't know.

Jorgen   I do – that's how I play the tortured husband role so well.

Hedda   I'd rather crash my car into a man than marry one –

Jorgen   Nobody says you have to choose.

Hedda   I need to talk to him – Henrik – about the script. I asked my agent, weeks ago, to send a copy but –

Jorgen   Your agent isn't answering your calls.

Hedda   They're acting like I've killed someone –

Jorgen   He didn't die? The paparazzi?

Hedda   No. Just – maimed. Just – lightly maimed.

Jorgen *smiles, finishing his cigarette.*

Jorgen   You know it's not your agent's fault you have no script –

Hedda   Why's that?

Jorgen   There is no script.

Two

Hedda *and* **Thea***'s trailer.* **Thea** *is at the mirror – make-up arranged in neat rows.* **Hedda** *sweeps it aside to make room – knocking it to the floor.*

Hedda   Sorry – did I knock your –

Hedda *leans down to pick up* **Thea***'s make-up. As she hands it back:*

Hedda   You shouldn't use that – awful for your skin.

Thea   I haven't had a problem with it –

Hedda   You haven't? No – your skin looks – fine. You saw him then?

Thea   Saw who?

Hedda   Our fearless leader –

Thea   Jonas Gahr Støre?

Hedda   Who?

Thea   Norway's prime minister –

Hedda   I mean Henrik –

Thea   I know you do – and yes, I saw him –

Hedda   And is he still appreciative of your technique?

Thea *holds* **Hedda***'s gaze – then laughs, dismissively.*

Thea   You're nervous about working with him –

Hedda   Why would I be nervous?

Thea   You haven't worked with somebody like him before.

Hedda   How do you know?

Thea   Because there is no one like him in the world. He is a genius –

Hedda   And genius is code for?

Hedda *smiles* – **Thea** *does not.*

Thea   You haven't played Hedda before?

Hedda   Have you?

Thea   At the academy. Although I was too young –

Hedda   Maybe they thought that you seemed old. It's your severity – it makes you seem mature –

Thea   You've read the play?

Hedda   I skimmed it – on the plane –

Thea   And did you understand the play?

Hedda   I – liked it –

Thea   That's not what I asked. The play depicts a woman's realisation she is trapped – by her marriage, her gender, her financial circumstances. By her fear, her nervousness –

Hedda   She isn't nervous –

Thea   No? Then what?

Hedda   She's – desperate –

Thea   For what?

Hedda   Escape. From marriage – domesticity – from men –

Thea   Which men?

Hedda   Her husband, Jorgen –

Thea   An unimpressive man – a safe option –

Hedda   She doesn't want safety. Or she wants to want it, but –

Thea   There is another man she wants – Ejlert, her lover –

Hedda   He's not her lover anymore –

Thea   What happened?

Hedda   Just – what happens. It – ended. Not well.

Thea   He comes to tell her of his work –

Hedda   A manuscript –

Thea   She burns it –

Hedda   Good for her.

Thea   Why does she burn it?

Hedda   Maybe she just wants to destroy something. A manuscript, a man – herself –

Thea   So you have read it then? So you know how it ends –

Hedda   With – death.

Thea   With Hedda's death.

Hedda   Days after coming home from honeymoon – Hedda is dead.

Thea   She kills herself –

Hedda   I know –

Thea   So – say that then.

Hedda   She kills herself.

Thea   Why does she kill herself?

Hedda   I – don't know –

Thea   You don't.

Hedda   Not yet.

Thea   And there's another man – neither the husband nor the lover –

Hedda   Brack –

Thea   A man with money – power. A man who likes to use his power to make other people – women – powerless –

Hedda   A man like that? Must be a work of fiction –

Berta *enters. To* **Hedda***:*

Berta   He can see you now.

Three

On set. **Hedda** *and* **Henrik** *stand, facing each other.*

Henrik   You don't look how I thought you would.

Hedda   We met –

Henrik   Online – it's not the same as in the flesh.

Hedda   Well – here I am. My – flesh. And I am – so excited. It's a – dream come true. But I do have – questions –

Henrik   Questions?

Hedda   Yes – about the script –

Henrik   There is no script.

Hedda   My questions are about the lack of script. I thought –

Henrik   That there would be a script?

Hedda   I –

Henrik   You're uncomfortable –

Hedda   With you?

Henrik   Without a script. It's fine with me, if you're uncomfortable –

Hedda   I'm not. It's just – it isn't what I'm used to –

Henrik   No one is asking you to play the prom queen here.

Hedda   I'm twenty years too old to play a prom queen –

Henrik   So – time for suicide.

Hedda   You've watched my movies then?

Henrik   Are you surprised?

Hedda   You're not the target audience.

Henrik   That doesn't mean I got no pleasure from them.

Hedda You enjoyed them?

Henrik Sometimes multiple times.

Hedda You're trying to make me feel uncomfortable –

Henrik Perhaps you'd like something to help you relax –

Hedda A drink?

Henrik Unless there's something else you had in mind.

Henrik *pours drinks. He offers one to* **Hedda**.

Hedda No thanks – I'm here to work –

Henrik You're here – so all of this is work.

Hedda You don't think it's a bit cliché? Auteur director – drinking whisky, trying to intimidate people –

Henrik So you're intimidated by me?

Hedda I said trying to.

Henrik But you do think I'm an auteur. A genius –

Hedda I didn't use that word.

Henrik The auteur and the child star –

Hedda I'm not a child star. That was – before –

Henrik And now?

Hedda I'm – more than that. I can be more than that. A serious actor –

Henrik I didn't bring you here to be an actor. I brought you here to show me something – give me something –

Hedda What?

Henrik The truth. That's why there is no script – so there is nothing you can hide behind. Or did you come out here to hide?

Hedda I came because – I hit something. A block. A wall –

Henrik   A photographer.

Hedda   You heard? But you still hired me –

Henrik   That's why I hired you. It was an accident? Tell me the truth –

Hedda   The truth is – I don't know.

Henrik   Sometimes these things can happen – when there is no script.

Hedda   You're interested in danger –

Henrik   I am interested in truth. Not in performance – acting – in the tricks you do. You're not a dog – so please, don't act like one.

Hedda   I'm not a dog –

Henrik   That's what I said – you're not a dog.

Hedda   What are you trying to do –

Henrik   I'm trying to work.

Hedda   Me too. I'm here to work – no drama –

Henrik   Not easy, when it is a drama – or do you think that Hedda Gabler is a comedy?

Hedda   She kills herself to get away from men – what could be funnier than that?

Henrik   You're here to work – so I will tell you how it works. I give you a scenario – a world you can exist inside. You have your role – our task now is to excavate that individual. Remove the separation, between them and you – until you can become. Not merely seem to be – but be. That's all I ask of you – to be.

Hedda   Be –

Henrik   Hedda Gabler.

Hedda   I can do it –

Henrik   Good – then do.

Hedda *holds* **Henrik***'s gaze – then takes the second glass.*
She drinks.

Henrik   Welcome home, Hedda.

Four

On set. **Hedda** *enters.* **Jorgen, Thea** *and* **Berta** *are waiting*
for her.

Jorgen   Here –

Jorgen *holds out his hand to* **Hedda** *– in it is a 1,000 kroner note.*

Hedda   What's this?

Jorgen   For you. We had a bet.

Hedda   What bet?

Thea   That you would leave after you met with Henrik –
run away –

Hedda   You thought that I'd be scared away?

Thea   We both did –

Hedda   But I wasn't –

Jorgen   No. So – it's for you.

Hedda   A thousand kroner? That's a lot?

Jorgen   Maybe enough to get a taxi to the airport – if you
change your mind about running away.

Henrik *enters.* **Thea, Jorgen, Berta** *and* **Hedda** *turn to him.*

Henrik   It begins in Norway, just outside of Oslo – but
inland, not by the sea. The feeling is of suffocation,
claustrophobia – a house, with thick stone walls. A woman,
Hedda, sits upon a sofa –

Hedda   Should I – sit down –

Henrik   Is this Beginners Acting 101? She sits – the woman, Hedda – in her home. Her new home – new husband sat beside her –

Jorgen   Should I –

Henrik *nods.* **Jorgen** *moves closer to* **Hedda**.

Henrik   They're newlyweds – does that say newlyweds to you?

Jorgen *moves closer – touching* **Hedda** *now. She shifts, uncomfortable.*

Henrik   He touches her. Her body. Skin. She tenses and he says:

Jorgen   You're nervous –

Hedda   No –

Jorgen   There's something on your mind.

Hedda   It's just –

Henrik   She starts to speak – he interrupts. He says:

Jorgen   It's my promotion, isn't it? You're worried it won't happen –

Hedda   That isn't what is on her mind –

Henrik   What is?

Thea   Her body –

Henrik   Yes – her body. What about her body?

Thea   How it's changing – ageing –

Hedda   No –

Thea   She's in denial –

Henrik   Yes. Denial about what?

Hedda   You're asking me?

Henrik   Of course – you do play Hedda Gabler –

Hedda   I do – I just – I thought –

Henrik   Touch her –

Hedda   Touch me?

Again, **Jorgen** *reaches for* **Hedda**. *She tenses, but accepts his touch.*

Henrik   And tell me how she's changed.

Jorgen   She's – different. Than she was.

Thea   She's put on weight –

Hedda   I haven't –

Henrik   She denies it, but you know she has –

Hedda   I'm sorry – can we – stop?

Henrik   We cannot stop. What else?

Thea   Another woman –

Henrik   Thea. She is – what?

Thea   Younger than Hedda – slimmer –

Hedda   Not by much –

Thea   Enough.

Henrik   Enough to what?

Thea   To make her jealous –

Hedda   Please – she isn't jealous –

Henrik   No? Or are you scared to admit jealousy? Afraid to say what makes you insecure –

Hedda   You're asking me? Or Hedda?

Henrik   There should not be a separation, between her and you.

Hedda   I –

Henrik   No. Somebody else. You – Jorgen. Tell me –

Jorgen   Yes?

Henrik   About your jealousy. About what makes you insecure.

Hedda   You're asking him? Or Jorgen?

Henrik   I am asking him – not you. What makes you insecure?

Jorgen   I fear that I will always be the second choice. The husband, not the lover – somebody undesired, easily dismissed –

Henrik   And is he – Jorgen – is he undesired?

Henrik *waits for* **Hedda** *or* **Thea** *to answer. An awkward silence, then:*

Hedda   No – he's –

Henrik   No? Okay – so –

Hedda   What?

Henrik   So show him –

Hedda   Show him what?

Henrik   How you desire him.

Hedda *stares at* **Henrik** *– then turns to* **Jorgen***. She kisses him, lightly.*

Henrik   That's your desire? Please – you're not a child actor anymore.

Hedda   What are you asking for?

Henrik   I want to see something that I believe.

Hedda   You want to see us fuck?

Henrik   If that is what you want to show me – go ahead. Please. Fuck.

Hedda *looks between* **Henrik** *and* **Jorgen** *in disbelief – then laughs.*

Hedda   No –

Henrik   Why?

Hedda   I – don't want to –

Henrik   Why?

Hedda   Because – I don't.

Henrik   Why not?

Hedda   I – don't desire him. I can't desire him. I'm sorry –

Henrik   Don't apologise. This is our work.

Hedda   So this is how it works? You ask us to degrade each other – to degrade ourselves –

Henrik   I want you to reveal yourself – if you find that degrading, that is up to you.

Hedda   And when I have – revealed myself –

Henrik   If you are able to –

Hedda   When do we shoot?

Henrik   When we are all prepared to shoot. When you have given me enough to write, then I will write – and then we shoot.

Hedda   And how much – is enough –

Henrik   I'll tell you when it is enough. Now – you tell me.

Hedda   Tell you –

Henrik   The truth.

Hedda *hesitates.* **Henrik** *watches her, intently – a test.*

Hedda   The truth – is that it's only been a day. Since she arrived – since I arrived – to this new home. But it – it doesn't feel like home. And I already – I feel trapped. Regretful. Unprepared.

Henrik   Afraid –

Hedda   Afraid, yes. Of what happens next. Of what I will do next.

Henrik   You die.

Hedda   I die.

Henrik   You kill yourself.

Hedda   I do –

Henrik   Say it –

Hedda   I kill myself. Days after she – no, I – arrive – I kill myself.

Henrik   You're shaking. Why?

Hedda   I'm cold – it's cold –

Henrik   It's Norway –

Hedda   And it's fucking cold.

Henrik   That isn't why you're shaking –

Hedda   Yes, it is –

Henrik   It isn't –

Hedda   No –

Henrik   Why are you shaking?

Hedda   Because I – I –

Henrik   Enough.

Hedda   Enough?

Henrik   For now. I have to write – tomorrow we will shoot the opening –

Berta   Except the scenes with Brack. Brack is –

Hedda   Brack is another man – a man with money, power –

Berta   Please – don't interrupt. Brack is in hospital –

Hedda   In hospital?

Henrik   It doesn't matter if he is in hospital – it only matters that he is not here. And so – we start without him. And when we do – we do not stop. Until I tell you 'cut'.

Hedda   And if you don't say 'cut'?

Henrik   Then you don't stop.

Henrik *exits –* **Thea** *and* **Jorgen** *follow.* **Hedda** *exhales.*

Hedda   Is he always like that?

Berta   Henrik? That's how he works –

Hedda   And does it work?

Berta   Some people think he is a genius –

Hedda   And you think?

Berta   He's a man who likes control. You know he used to be an actor? But then he realised that actors – they have no control.

Hedda   I have control –

Berta   That's good you feel that way – but I'm not here to talk about the way you feel. Although there are resources here for that –

Hedda   What resources?

Berta   We are a small crew – another way that Henrik keeps control – but we do have an on-set therapist –

Hedda   I don't need a therapist –

Berta   Again – that's good you feel that way.

Five

On set. **Hedda**, **Jorgen** *and* **Thea** *sit, each with a glass of wine – next to* **Hedda** *is a wine bottle.* **Jorgen** *scrolls on his phone.* **Henrik** *watches.*

Berta   Ready?

Henrik *nods.* **Jorgen** *puts his phone in his pocket and picks up his glass.*

Berta   Rolling. Sound speed. Mark it – action.

Thea   Congratulations.

Hedda   Are congratulations in order?

Thea   Your wedding. I heard it was charming – intimate –

Hedda   Hardly – I could barely move for being looked at –

Thea   Most people get married because they want to be looked at.

Hedda   You're wondering why you weren't invited?

Thea   You're wondering why I've turned up at your home. You first.

Hedda   I don't like your husband – I didn't want him at my wedding –

Thea   I don't like him either – I should never have had him at mine.

Jorgen   You've left your husband? I'm sorry – that sounds painful –

Hedda   I think it might be more painful to stay.

Hedda *and* **Thea** *laugh –* **Jorgen** *does not.*

Thea   Your house is beautiful. Enormous. Can you afford it?

Hedda   Jorgen is getting a promotion. At the university.

Jorgen   And if I don't, she'll leave me –

Hedda   Yes – I will –

Jorgen   I'm joking –

Hedda   So am I. More wine?

Jorgen You're sure, darling? More wine?

Hedda I do apologise – my husband's quite controlling –

Jorgen No – I'm just – concerned. Drinking – in your condition –

Hedda What condition? Being bored to death?

Jorgen I wish you wouldn't say that you were bored so much –

Hedda Would you prefer I lie?

Jorgen I didn't think that you were capable –

Hedda You don't know what I'm capable of.

Henrik Cut. Now, go again – but find more violence this time –

Hedda You mean – metaphorically –

Henrik What else?

Berta From where?

Henrik Your house is beautiful –

Berta Rolling. Sound speed. Mark it – action.

Thea Your house is beautiful. Enormous. Can you afford it?

Hedda Jorgen is getting a promotion. At the university.

Jorgen And if I don't, she'll leave me –

Hedda Yes – I will –

Jorgen I'm joking –

Hedda So am I. More wine?

Jorgen You're sure, darling? More wine?

Hedda I do apologise – my husband's quite controlling –

Jorgen   No – I'm just – concerned. Drinking – in your condition –

Hedda   What condition? Being bored to death?

Jorgen   I wish you wouldn't say that you were bored so much –

Hedda   Would you prefer I lie?

Jorgen   I didn't think that you were capable –

Hedda   You don't know what I'm capable of.

Henrik   Cut. Again – more violence. From Jorgen's line – I didn't think that you were capable –

Berta   Rolling. Sound speed. Mark it – action.

Jorgen   I didn't think that you were capable –

Hedda   You don't know what I'm capable of.

Henrik   Keep rolling – give me Hedda's line again –

Hedda   You don't know what I'm capable of.

Henrik   I don't believe you. Again –

Hedda   You don't know what I'm capable of –

Henrik   I don't believe you – again –

Hedda   You don't know what I'm capable of –

Henrik   Again –

Hedda   You don't know what I'm capable of –

Henrik   Again!

Hedda   You don't know what I'm capable of!

A moment. **Hedda** *waits for* **Henrik**'s *response – but he remains silent.*

Hedda   Enough? Is that – enough?

Berta   More wine –

Hedda   Sorry?

Henrik   Your line – more wine –

Hedda   Are we – still rolling?

Henrik   Did I tell you 'cut'?

Hedda *blinks – frozen for a moment – then refills the wine glasses.*

Hedda   More wine –

Thea   Please. I find with certain wines, they don't get drinkable until you're three or four drinks in –

Jorgen   Did you come here for a reason? Or just to denigrate my wine?

Thea   And cause friction in your marriage. And announce that Ejlert –

Hedda   Ejlert?

Thea   He's come back – to the university –

Hedda   Ejlert's come back?

Jorgen   But – he was fired from the university – his drinking –

Thea   That's all in the past –

Jorgen   And now?

Thea   He's back –

Jorgen   But why?

Thea   Maybe he's heard there's a promotion going –

Jorgen   But – that's my promotion –

Thea   But now Ejlert's back –

Jorgen   You think he's going to steal my job from me?

Hedda   Unless there's something else for him to steal.

Jorgen   Like what?

Hedda   Some men do have desires outside their employment –

Jorgen   I have – desires –

Hedda   Please, Jorgen – not in front of guests.

Hedda *and* **Thea** *laugh.* **Jorgen** *reaches for the wine bottle.*

Jorgen   I think I'll have another glass –

Hedda   Are you sure, darling? More wine?

Jorgen   Give me the wine.

Again, **Jorgen** *reaches for the bottle – but* **Hedda** *holds it out of reach.*

Jorgen   Give me the wine.

Henrik   Give him the wine –

Hedda *offers* **Jorgen** *the bottle.*

Henrik   Not like that –

Jorgen   Give me the wine.

Hedda *starts to tip the bottle to refill* **Jorgen***'s glass.*

Henrik   No –

Jorgen   Give me the wine.

Hedda *lifts the bottle towards* **Jorgen***'s mouth.*

Henrik   No –

Jorgen   Give me the wine.

Hedda *hesitates, then empties the bottle over* **Jorgen***.* **Henrik** *smiles.*

Hedda   I'll get another bottle, shall I?

Henrik   Cut! Good –

Hedda   Thanks –

Henrik   It's not a compliment. It's your job.

Henrik *exits, followed by* **Berta**. **Jorgen** *is silent – furious.*

Thea   I'm going to change my clothes – you spilled a little wine on me.

Thea *exits.* **Hedda** *approaches* **Jorgen**, *cautiously.*

Hedda   So – that went well –

Jorgen   Did it?

Hedda   You heard him – he said good –

Jorgen   To you. So – it was good for you.

Hedda   We work together –

Jorgen   So how come you're not soaked in wine?

Jorgen *takes out his phone from his pocket – it is broken.*

Jorgen   Fuck! My fucking phone –

Hedda   I didn't mean to –

Jorgen   Yes, you did. You poured the wine on me and broke my phone.

Hedda   He told me to –

Jorgen   And? Do you do everything he says?

Hedda   No. But – we were shooting –

Jorgen   And? I've worked with Henrik for a decade – been humiliated countless times. You think he ever tells you it's enough? That what you've given is enough? You think you can pass his test – you can't. There's always more.

Hedda   I will. I can. I want to prove that he was right to choose me –

Jorgen   Choose you? No – he didn't choose. He sent an offer out to every washed-up actor in the northern hemisphere. And before that – every not washed-up one too. No one replied. You did

Hedda   I don't believe you.

Jorgen   Now you sound like him.

Hedda   I do?

Jorgen   It's not a compliment.

Six

On set. **Berta** *is alone – on the phone.*

> **Berta**   *Can I speak to him? I know – I know he gets upset – but please, just let me speak to him. For fuck's sake – let me talk to him –*

A sudden shift in **Berta***'s tone – still on the phone.*

> **Berta**   *Hi, sweetie – how are you? I know – I missed you too. I know – I said that I'd be home. But that's not how work works. So –*

Another shift in **Berta***'s tone.*

> **Berta**   *Hey – I'm talking to him – I was talking to him, trying to explain. Okay – I'll see you later, then. No – I don't know what time –*

The other speaker hangs up. **Berta** *shuts her eyes.* **Hedda** *enters.*

Hedda   Are you okay?

Berta   I'm fine. It's – fine. It's – scheduling. Henrik – he likes to take his time. He doesn't understand his time is other people's lives. And now we've heard Brack must remain in hospital. We have to find another actor – which means more delay. I hate delay.

Hedda   I meant to ask you – about casting –

Berta   Yes?

Hedda   About – my role –

Hedda *hesitates.* **Berta** *waits for her to continue.*

Berta   Please – I just said I hate delay –

Hedda   I wondered who's been cast to play my lover – my ex-lover –

Berta   Ejlert? Henrik hasn't told you?

Hedda   No –

Berta   A movie star –

Hedda   Which one?

Berta   This one.

Berta *shows* **Hedda** *a photo of* **Ejlert** *on her phone.* **Hedda** *is stunned.*

Hedda   But – him – I know him –

Berta   Yes – he is a movie star –

Hedda   I mean – I know him. Used to know him. He's my ex –

Henrik *enters.* **Hedda** *turns to him, incredulous.*

Hedda   You've cast my ex? To play my ex? But that's –

Henrik   A stroke of genius?

Hedda   I wouldn't use that word.

Henrik   This casting gives us truth – a layer of reality –

Hedda   It makes it weird.

Henrik   Reality is weird. Your lover –

Hedda   Ex –

Henrik   Arrives tomorrow. And we will have our Brack –

Berta   You've recast Brack?

Henrik   I have.

Hedda   And who is that?

Henrik   Another man you know –

Hedda   Who?

Henrik   Me.

Act Two

Seven

On set. **Hedda** *and* **Henrik** *face each other – he holds a gun.*

Henrik   We are alone – Hedda and Brack. In Norway, just outside of Oslo – in the house I paid for –

Hedda   House Brack paid for –

Henrik   House I bought for you –

Hedda   You bought it for my husband –

Henrik   No – I bought this house for you. Why did I do that?

Hedda   Because – you're generous –

Henrik   I'm not.

Hedda   Because – you want something –

Henrik   I do –

Hedda   And what is that?

Henrik *offers the gun to* **Hedda**. *She accepts it, cautiously.*

Hedda   What's this?

Henrik   It's yours – you're holding it when I arrive.

Hedda   I've seen you coming –

Henrik   Or – you didn't notice me. How does it feel?

Hedda   It's heavy –

Henrik   It's a gun. You've held a gun before?

Hedda   What makes you think that?

Henrik   You're American. How does it feel?

Hedda   To be American?

Henrik   To hold a gun. Do you feel nervous?

Hedda   No –

Henrik   What then?

Hedda   I feel – powerful. Does that make you uncomfortable? I don't mind if you're uncomfortable –

Henrik   I'm not uncomfortable –

Hedda   How about now?

Hedda *raises the gun – pointing it at* **Henrik**. *He smiles.*

Hedda   Your turn to tell the truth – was I your first choice for this role?

Henrik   My first choice for this role is dead. So – lucky you.

Hedda   She's dead?

Henrik   Why would I make that up?

Hedda   But you think I can do it –

Henrik   Do you think you can?

Hedda   I – yes. I can. I am.

Henrik   What?

Hedda   I am Hedda Gabler –

Henrik   I don't believe you –

Hedda   I am Hedda Gabler –

Henrik   No –

Hedda   I am Hedda Gabler. I am Hedda Gabler.

Hedda *moves closer to* **Henrik**, *still aiming the gun at him.*

Hedda   I – am.

Hedda *fires. A gunshot.* **Berta** *enters – rushing to* **Hedda** *to take the gun.*

Berta   What are you doing – fuck – you want to hurt someone?

Hedda   How can I hurt him – it's a prop gun –

Berta   It's dangerous. It fires blanks, not bullets – but even blanks, from close enough, can – *decimate* –

Henrik   Decimate –

Berta   Decimate the body. Decimate the skin. You put it in your mouth and pull the trigger – it will kill you. It can kill you. Understand?

Hedda   I didn't put it in my mouth –

Berta   You do not handle it without me here. You understand?

Henrik   She's asking – do you understand?

Hedda   I – do. But I – it's not my fault. I didn't get the gun.

Henrik   Who did?

Hedda   You did. You got the gun. Were holding it when I arrived.

Berta   Henrik? You know that it's my job to get the gun –

Henrik   It is – but you were late.

Berta   I'm sorry, but – my son –

Henrik   Is your son working on this film? No? Then I don't want to know. Now – give her back the gun –

Berta   I have to – first – complete some paperwork –

Henrik   Give her the gun –

Berta   Some safety protocols –

Henrik   Give her the gun!

Berta *hesitates, then relents – handing* **Hedda** *the gun. Condescendingly:*

Henrik   You have some paperwork?

Berta – *humiliated* – *hands a piece of paper to* **Hedda**.

Berta   A waiver. To declare you take responsibility for any harm –

Hedda   What harm?

Berta   There won't be any harm. But if there is – it's a formality, that's all. Also I have to ask some questions for our liability – you aren't under the influence of drugs or alcohol?

Hedda   I'm not –

Berta   Are not feeling coerced? Forced to behave in certain ways?

Hedda   I – no.

Berta   You don't have concerns with your mental health? Not feeling anxious? Insecure? As though your life is not in your control?

Hedda   I'm an actress on a movie set. So yes – to all of the above.

Berta   It's serious –

Hedda   I'm being serious.

Berta   If you don't answer 'no', we cannot go ahead –

Hedda   Then no – I do not feel coerced to act in certain ways.

Berta   Sign here. And – just to check – you aren't pregnant?

Hedda   Pregnant? Why would you ask me that?

Berta   It's a formality – for the waiver. But – you're not –

Hedda   I'm – no. Of course I'm not.

Henrik   She is –

Hedda   What?

Henrik   Pregnant –

Hedda   No – I'm not –

Henrik   Hedda is. And you are Hedda – but you aren't –

Hedda   Pregnant? No –

Henrik   That would be too perfect, wouldn't it? How would you feel?

Hedda   If – I was pregnant? Now? I would be – terrified –

Henrik   Why?

Hedda   Because I wouldn't – if I was – was pregnant – I wouldn't be ready – wouldn't feel ready –

Henrik   But you're not so young –

Hedda   No. But – I still feel young – too young –

Henrik   Just say that you don't want a child.

Hedda   I – don't know. I – sometimes, maybe –

Berta   No.

Henrik *and* **Hedda** *turn to* **Berta** *– surprised by her interruption. Stilted:*

Berta   I just meant that – a child isn't something you can want sometimes.

Henrik   And – you are –

Berta   I'm – what?

Henrik   I'm asking you what character you play?

Berta   I'm – not an actor – I'm the first AD –

Henrik   Of course – you get the gun. You do the paperwork.

Berta   I do –

Henrik   So don't you have some paperwork to do?

Berta   I'm sorry – I just thought – I'm a parent. I have a child – I know what it's like. I thought – that I could contribute –

Henrik   I said already – I don't want to hear about your son.

Berta   Okay. I – understand.

Henrik   And you apologise?

Berta   I – apologise. I was just trying to contribute –

Henrik   Don't.

Henrik *exits.* **Hedda** *turns to* **Berta.**

Hedda   I'm sorry –

Berta   Don't apologise – it's fine. It's my job –

Hedda   To let him treat you like that?

Berta   You think it's worse than he treats you?

Berta *takes the gun from* **Hedda,** *then turns to exit.* **Hedda** *calls after her.*

Hedda   What you said – about a child being something that you have to want forever, not sometimes – it made me feel –

Berta   I'm sorry –

Hedda   Don't apologise –

Berta   I have to go. I have a job to do. My job here's not to talk about the way you feel. I told you that we have an on-set therapist –

Hedda   But I don't need a therapist –

Berta   You need someone to talk to. And that's not my job.

Eight

A private space. **Thea** *sits, hands clasped.* **Hedda** *stares at her, confused.*

Thea   So – you need some help.

Hedda   Sorry –

Thea   There's no need to apologise –

Hedda   I'm just –

Thea   Do you apologise a lot?

Hedda   Confused –

Thea   You feel confused a lot?

Hedda   You're – the therapist?

Thea   I am. And can I ask you why you feel confused? Perhaps you think because I'm young and female and conventionally attractive, I can't be qualified for such a role?

Hedda   I'm confused because – you're an actor –

Thea   Most actors have a second job. For me – it's therapy.

Hedda   But you can't be the therapist on-set – when you're on-set –

Thea   Makes sense to me – I'm here already –

Hedda   But there's a conflict –

Thea   It's a drama – conflict is built-in. So – where shall we begin? Perhaps let's start with your internalised misogyny –

Hedda   This isn't – no – it's not appropriate –

Thea   It's a safe space –

Hedda   I don't feel safe –

Thea   No? Do you feel nervous? Scared?

Hedda   Did Henrik say to say that – that I'm scared –

Thea   There's that misogyny again. My role here's not for Henrik – it's to offer you support. Support I see you really need. How long have you had struggles with your mental health? Is there a trauma you would like to share? Do you find that your sense of self is malleable? Only feel real when you're observed?

Hedda   I don't want to be observed, don't want to be so fucking seen –

Thea   Most people don't get into acting, if they don't want to be seen.

Hedda   I just feel like – he's watching me – Henrik –

Thea   You think that Henrik's watching you? Right now?

Hedda   I don't mean like he's watching through the mirror –

Thea   But he could be – couldn't he?

Hedda *turns to stare into the mirror.* **Thea** *watches her.*

Thea   Perhaps we ought to talk about your paranoid beliefs –

Hedda   I'm – not. Not paranoid, not insecure, not anxious, not coerced – not pregnant –

Thea   Wow. We should arrange another time to talk – it seems we have a great deal to discuss –

Hedda   There's nothing to discuss – I'm here to work –

Thea   So let's discuss your work –

Hedda   My work is fine. I'm fine. I just –

Thea   What?

Hedda   I want to give him what he wants. To prove I can –

Thea   Can what?

Hedda   Can be. Her. Hedda Gabler.

Thea   And if you can become her – what happens to you?

Hedda   I – disappear –

Thea   And is that what you want?

Nine

On set. **Henrik** *and* **Berta** *wait for* **Hedda**. *She enters under the following:*

> **Henrik**   *In therapy? You sent her to therapy? She's here to be my Hedda Gabler – you think Hedda Gabler went to therapy?*

Hedda   I think maybe if Hedda Gabler had gone to therapy, there might have been a different ending.

Henrik   Oh – you speak Norwegian now? You're late –

Hedda   I was –

Henrik   At therapy. You are unhappy?

Hedda   No – I'm fine –

Henrik   Good – then let's start. You like it here.

Hedda   I said – I'm fine.

Henrik   It's not a question – it's my line.

Berta   Rolling. Sound speed. Mark it – action.

Henrik   You like it here? The house?

Hedda   You paid for it –

Henrik   I did –

Hedda   It wouldn't be polite to not say yes.

Henrik   Good girl.

Hedda   I'm not your girl.

Henrik   You aren't included in the price?

Hedda   What price?

Henrik *approaches* **Hedda**, *moving to kiss her. She backs away.*

Hedda   Sorry –

Henrik   That's not your line –

Hedda   I just –

Henrik   We're rolling – and that's not the line –

Hedda   What is the line –

Berta   There is no line. He kisses you –

Hedda   He – what –

Henrik   It's in the script –

Hedda   It isn't in my script –

Henrik   You must not have the latest script –

Hedda   So can I see the latest script?

Henrik   We're rolling –

Hedda   Let me see the script!

Henrik   Fine – fuck. Cut.

Henrik *scowls as* **Berta** *approaches* **Hedda**, *with a copy of the script.*

Hedda   What does that mean – forcefully – it says here you kiss me –

Henrik   I don't kiss you – Brack does –

Hedda   Forcefully –

Henrik   Maybe it's easier if I just show you. So – let's go again –

Hedda   Hold on –

Henrik   It wouldn't be polite to not say yes.

Berta   Rolling. Sound speed. Mark it. Action.

Hedda   It – wouldn't be polite to not say yes –

Henrik   Good girl.

Hedda   I'm not your girl.

Henrik   You aren't included in the price?

Hedda   What price?

Henrik *approaches* **Hedda**, *forcefully. Again, she backs away.*

Berta   Cut!

     Henrik   *You don't say 'cut' – I say 'cut' –*

Berta   I know but – she seemed scared –

Henrik   She's acting – aren't you?

Hedda   It – wouldn't be polite to not say yes.

Henrik   Good girl.

Hedda   I'm not your girl.

Berta   I'm sorry – are we shooting –

Henrik *ignores* **Berta** *– kissing* **Hedda**, *roughly. She pushes him off.*

Hedda   I'm not doing this –

Henrik   It's your job –

Hedda   And I'm not doing it like this.

Berta   Perhaps I'll call the intimacy co-ordinator –

Hedda   There's an intimacy co-ordinator?

Berta   Yes – we are a small crew here, but –

Hedda   Get the fucking intimacy co-ordinator. Now. Fuck. Please.

Berta *exits.* **Henrik** *and* **Hedda** *are alone.*

Henrik   It's just a kiss – it isn't intimate –

Hedda   You don't decide what's intimate –

Henrik   I'll take it as a compliment you feel so intimate with me.

Berta *re-enters, with* **Thea**.

Hedda   What's she doing here?

Thea   You're shooting something intimate –

Hedda   So what – you're here to watch? I want a closed set. Just us – and the intimacy co-ordinator –

Thea   I am the intimacy co-ordinator.

Hedda   You? Seriously?

Thea   What? Just because I'm young and female and –

Berta   They need to kiss.

Thea   Okay – so kiss –

Berta   The script says that it should be forceful –

Henrik   Violent –

Berta   My script doesn't use that word –

Henrik   Then please – update your script.

Thea   Violent, okay. So – shall we have a go?

Henrik *kisses* **Hedda** *violently. She struggles – then submits.*

Henrik   Like that?

Thea   If that is what you want – you're the director, after all.

Henrik   That's what I want. So please – let's go again.

Berta   From where?

Henrik   Good girl.

Ten

Hedda *and* **Thea**'s *trailer.* **Hedda** *is alone. A knock at the door.*

Hedda   Can I have one fucking moment, please?

Ejlert   Sure thing.

Hedda *opens the door –* **Ejlert** *enters.*

Hedda   It's – you.

Ejlert   It's you. Are you – okay?

Hedda   I'm fine.

Ejlert   You don't look fine – come here –

Hedda   I said I'm fine –

Ejlert   I said – come here.

Hedda *relents –* **Ejlert** *embraces her. A moment – then she pulls away.*

Hedda   Why are you here?

Ejlert   I'm playing Ejlert –

Hedda   Ejlert – but why?

Ejlert   We all need work.

Hedda   Not you – the movie star –

Ejlert   Please – you're the movie star –

Hedda   I'm almost unemployable – but you're in everything –

Ejlert   Have you seen any of it?

Hedda   On a plane, maybe.

Ejlert *laughs. Some sense of how they used to be.*

Hedda   It's been a while –

Ejlert   You still look the same.

Hedda   As when I was eighteen? Don't lie –

Ejlert   I'm acting –

Hedda   They don't like that here.

In a Norwegian accent, mimicking **Henrik***:*

Hedda   I am not interested in acting. I am interested in truth.

Ejlert   I don't think I can do truth, anymore. I spend my life on green screen, acting opposite a tennis ball –

Hedda   You mean those weren't real dinosaurs?

Ejlert   I'm sorry – does that spoil it for you?

Hedda   So you didn't really punch a pterodactyl? But you did strangle a t-rex –

Ejlert   Those are two different movies –

Hedda   So?

Ejlert   So you must catch a lot of planes. Unless you're watching me destroy the dinosaurs at home –

Hedda   What home? I have a suitcase and a storage space –

Ejlert   You like to travel –

Hedda   Did I say I liked it?

Ejlert   So – what are you doing here in Norway? If you didn't come here for your love of travel –

Hedda   Like you – I needed work –

Ejlert   That's all?

Hedda   And – I don't know. I wanted – needed – change –

Ejlert   And have you? Changed?

Hedda   Have you?

Ejlert   A lot. I'm sober now – I meditate, I'm vegan –

Hedda   Vegan? Seriously?

Ejlert   I don't joke about my health. When things have been that bad –

Hedda   Did things get bad?

Ejlert   They did – you know they did –

Hedda   I heard. But still – I wasn't there –

Ejlert   You left –

Hedda   I'm sorry –

Ejlert   I don't blame you. You were young – you had a reputation to protect. You were the prom queen –

Hedda   Only on a movie screen. So many times I played the prom queen – but never really went to prom –

Ejlert   I would have taken you. I would have loved that – get dressed up. Slow dance. Then all alone back in the limousine –

Hedda   I don't think real-life proms have limousines –

Ejlert   I wouldn't know. But still – we can pretend –

Ejlert *reaches for* **Hedda** *– but she moves away.*

Hedda   Don't –

Ejlert   I'm sorry – I thought – like we used to –

Hedda   That was back then. Now – it's now. We're not the same –

Ejlert   We could be –

Hedda   No –

Ejlert   I've missed you –

Hedda   Don't –

Ejlert   I always looked for you – at awards ceremonies, at parties –

Hedda   I didn't get invited to those parties. They're reserved for people who are taken seriously – not people who are jokes –

Ejlert   You're not a joke –

Hedda   I am. A make-up-smeared-no-underwear-and-passed-out-on-the-sidewalk joke. Too stupid to be taken seriously – but not fucked-up enough to just be left alone.

Ejlert   I heard about – the incident. The paparazzi – and the car –

Hedda   You saw the photo? Of the car, of the photographer – of me –

Ejlert   I did. I didn't try to, but –

Hedda   The photograph was everywhere – you didn't have to try.

Ejlert   It made me –

Hedda   What? It made you laugh?

Ejlert   It made me sad.

Hedda   That's worse.

Ejlert   If you need help –

Hedda   I don't need help.

Ejlert   I know – it's difficult to ask. I felt the same – but I can help. You asked me why I'm here – the truth is that I came to help you –

Hedda   I thought you came here to play Ejlert –

Ejlert   Please – I haven't even read the script –

Hedda   There is no script –

Ejlert   Then I don't feel bad for not reading it.

Hedda   You've never read the play?

Ejlert   What play?

Hedda   Hedda Gabler? By Henrik Ibsen?

Ejlert   Who the fuck is Henry Ibsen? No – I came out here
for you. I saw the photo and it made me sad. To see you look
so trapped – so helpless. So – please. Let me help.

Hedda   It isn't what you think – I've barely had a drink
since I arrived. The pills, the rest, all gone. That's not what I
need saving from.

Ejlert   But if I'm not here to save you – then why am I here?

Ejlert *moves closer to* **Hedda** *– this time she doesn't move away.*

Ejlert   We could go back to how we were. Why not?

Ejlert *and* **Hedda** *kiss. She undoes his shirt – then stops, noticing a
necklace around his neck. A sobriety chip, strung onto a thin gold
chain.*

Hedda   What's that?

Ejlert   My first year of sobriety –

Hedda   You didn't used to wear that –

Ejlert   I didn't use to be sober. It's not an issue, is it? That
I'm sober?

Hedda   It's just – different. You're different – so am I.
We've changed – both of us. We can't go back –

Ejlert   You're seeing someone else –

Hedda   I'm not –

Ejlert   I read it in a magazine –

Hedda   You read those magazines?

Ejlert   It was a long flight –

Hedda   Read a book –

Ejlert   You know I don't read books. It said you're dating –

Hedda   A director? That's all over –

Ejlert   No – an actor –

Hedda   Who?

Ejlert   Your husband – Jorgen –

Hedda   What? He's not my husband – and that's not his name. And we're not – no – we've barely met –

Ejlert   It's not the nineteenth century – you can be with someone you've barely met –

Hedda   You could back then – it's called an arranged marriage –

Ejlert   So that's what's going on – the studio have set you up?

Hedda   I think they're trying – yes – to set me up. They think they can control me – but they can't –

Ejlert   Prove it –

Hedda   Prove what?

Ejlert   That no one can control you –

Hedda   How?

Ejlert   Kiss me. Prove no one is controlling you and kiss me –

Hedda   No –

Hedda *pushes* **Ejlert** *away.* **Jorgen** *enters, carrying a bunch of flowers.*

Jorgen   These are for you –

Hedda   Has someone died?

Jorgen   You act as though you've not been taken on a date before –

Hedda   We do not have a date –

Jorgen   We do. Director's orders.

Jorgen *takes* **Hedda** *by the arm. As they exit,* **Ejlert** *shouts after them:*

Ejlert   I was lying – about coming here for you. I'm here for work! I'm here because I love my work! I love Hedda Gabler!

Hedda *and* **Jorgen** *are gone.* **Ejlert** *is alone.*

Ejlert   Fuck.

Eleven

Jorgen*'s trailer. He offers a chair to* **Hedda** *– but she remains standing.*

Jorgen   Sorry – were you expecting rose petals?

Hedda   Did Henrik put you up to this?

Jorgen   Of course – I am a married man –

Hedda   Unhappily married –

Jorgen   Yes – but I can be that on my own. You want a drink? I have –

Jorgen *gestures to a shelf filled with alcohol.*

Hedda   Pretty much everything –

Jorgen   Like you said – I'm an unhappy man.

Hedda   I'll have water –

Jorgen   Don't have water – second choice?

Hedda *doesn't reply –* **Jorgen** *pours them drinks. He drinks – she doesn't.*

Hedda   You have kids, don't you?

Jorgen   So you do take some interest in me –

Hedda   How old?

Jorgen   They're – three and – five – I think. Like this –

Jorgen *gestures around waist-height.*

Jorgen   And this.

Jorgen *gestures around knee-height.*

Hedda   You aren't around them much?

Jorgen   How can you tell?

Hedda   You love them?

Jorgen   They're my kids –

Hedda   But do you love them?

Jorgen   They're my kids. So – did I interrupt you? With the movie star?

Hedda   There was nothing to interrupt –

Jorgen   I have no need to be jealous then.

Hedda   You're jealous – seriously? Of him?

Jorgen   Of course. He's famous, handsome, rich – and childless, as far anybody knows. His jawline – has he had work done?

Hedda   He's had that jaw since we were both eighteen –

Jorgen   He knew you at eighteen – another reason for me to be jealous.

Hedda   Is Henrik sending you on dates with all the cast?

Jorgen   I'm not married to the rest of the cast –

Hedda   We're not married –

Jorgen   No – and Henrik thinks it's obvious. He wants us to be intimate – form a relationship. He says that we don't know each other –

Hedda   We don't.

Jorgen   So that's what we're doing now. Getting to know each other, asking each other personal questions – maybe later you might like to touch my knee. No? Okay – questions then. You first –

Hedda   Where were you born?

Jorgen   Outside the city. My turn – why don't you want to fuck me?

Hedda   What?

Jorgen   Another question – have you thought of suicide?

Hedda   Did Henrik say to ask me that?

Jorgen   He only asked for me to make you open up –

Hedda   And what if I don't want to open up?

Jorgen   Are you afraid of opening up?

Hedda   Just ask me – where I'm from –

Jorgen   Where are you from and why are you afraid of opening up?

Hedda   A small town, by the interstate. The light from the highway meant it never properly got dark. When I left home, I'd get so scared at night – being in darkness, in real darkness –

Jorgen   So – that's when you thought of suicide.

Hedda   It's my turn to ask a question. You're unhappy –

Jorgen   That's more of a comment than a question –

Hedda   Why?

Jorgen   Because – I'm impotent. Not physically – if it were physical, that would be fine. You take a pill – it's no big deal. But no – my impotence goes deeper. I'm ineffectual – powerless. I cannot get the things I want. You know I asked for Ejlert's part? And Brack's part, too? But Henrik told me no – I am a Jorgen. And he's right.

Hedda   You want to be somebody else – to change –

Jorgen   I want to be the movie star. I want to have what he has – fame, success, sobriety –

Hedda   You want sobriety?

Jorgen   Of course not – but I want to know I'd have the strength. But I already know – I'm weak. Weak and unhappy – just like you.

Hedda   I'm not weak –

Jorgen   But you are unhappy.

Hedda   Am I?

Jorgen   Please – it's obvious. You're cold and you are closed and you are running away. You are self-medicating – have been self-medicating – with drugs and alcohol and media attention. You came out here to change – but you won't change –

Hedda   I can –

Jorgen   No. You're fucked up – and fucked up people stay fucked up.

Hedda   You don't know me –

Jorgen   You don't know me –

Hedda   It that supposed to be my accent?

Jorgen   That's another thing I cannot do – an accent. Another way in which I'm impotent. I'm impotent in every fucking way except –

Jorgen *tries to make* **Hedda** *touch him – she pushes him off. As she exits:*

Jorgen   Go on then   run back to your movie star.

Twelve

On set. **Hedda** *and* **Ejlert** *face* **Henrik**. **Berta** *watches.*

Henrik   A woman, Hedda, sits upon a sofa – sat next to her, her lover –

Hedda   Ex-lover –

Henrik   From how long ago?

Ejlert   We haven't seen each other for a decade – longer –

Henrik   And now you're sitting in her husband's home. How does it feel?

Ejlert   To be sat here? With her? It feels – the same. Like it could be the same – like we could be the same –

Henrik *hands* **Hedda** *a photo.*

Hedda   What's this?

Henrik   A photo – of the two of you, when you first met –

Hedda   How do you have this?

Ejlert   Let me see. That's – wow. That's – us. We look – so young –

Henrik   What else?

Ejlert   She's beautiful –

Henrik   And him?

Hedda   He looks – how I remember him.

Henrik   And now?

Hedda   He's different –

Henrik   How?

Hedda   He's – had a life. It's been a – long time –

Henrik   And has she thought about him much, over this time?

Hedda Not much –

Ejlert He has.

Henrik About –

Ejlert Her – skin. Her smell. How she would look at him –

Hedda Stop it –

Henrik I'll tell you when to stop. Now tell me – when the two of you first met – what was she like?

Ejlert She was – an actor –

Henrik No – I don't mean that. I want to know about the first time that you fucked –

Hedda Excuse me?

Henrik I'm assuming you have fucked –

Ejlert We have –

Hedda Don't tell him that –

Henrik What was it like?

Hedda Please – do not tell him that.

Ejlert It's – work –

Hedda It's personal –

Henrik It's work.

Ejlert *stares at* **Hedda** *– then turns away from her, to* **Henrik**.

Ejlert We were eighteen. Just kids, really – but she seemed so grown-up. She smoked – gave me a cigarette. I didn't smoke – not then. I coughed – she laughed. She kissed me –

Hedda I'm not doing this –

Henrik You are. A cigarette –

Berta *hands* **Hedda** *a lit cigarette. She accepts it – but she doesn't smoke.*

Henrik   She smokes –

Hedda   No – I don't want to –

Henrik   Why?

Hedda   It makes me sick –

Ejlert   It never used to make you sick –

Hedda   I guess I've changed.

Henrik   Give it to him – the cigarette –

Hedda *passes* **Ejlert** *the cigarette. He takes a drag – then coughs.*

Henrik   Now – kiss.

Ejlert *leans in to kiss* **Hedda** *– but she pushes him away.*

Hedda   That isn't how it happened –

Henrik   No? What else?

Hedda   Drinks.

Henrik   Drinks –

Berta *brings on two glasses – hands them to* **Hedda** *and* **Ejlert.**

Henrik   The two of you – alone. With drinks. What happens next?

Hedda   She drinks.

Hedda *lifts the glass to her mouth. She drinks – then turns to* **Ejlert.**

Hedda   And he drinks too.

Ejlert *lifts the glass to his mouth – then hesitates.*

Ejlert   I'm sorry – is this alcohol? It's real?

Henrik   Of course –

Ejlert   I can't –

Hedda   It's work.

Ejlert   But what about my work – I'm sober – in recovery –

Hedda   This is your work.

Ejlert   And I take it seriously, but still – my health – my mental health –

Thea *enters. She approaches* **Ejlert**, *smiling widely.*

Thea   Did somebody say mental health?

As **Thea** *reaches out to shake* **Ejlert**'s *hand:*

Thea   On-set therapist, intimacy co-ordinator – and in love with you –

Ejlert   You're in love with me?

Thea   I am. I'm Thea – you are Ejlert –

Ejlert   I – don't understand.

Thea   I see that – so we have a lot of work to do. Henrik – you mind?

Henrik   Please – go ahead –

Thea *takes* **Ejlert**'s *hand – they exit.* **Hedda, Henrik** *and* **Berta** *remain.*

Henrik   You can go too –

Hedda   Me?

Henrik   No – not you.

Berta *hesitates – then exits. As she leaves, she makes a phone call:*

> **Berta**   *Hi, sweetie – go tell Daddy that I'm coming home –*

Henrik *crosses to* **Hedda**, *taking* **Ejlert**'s *place. He picks up a glass.*

Henrik   The two of us – alone. With drinks. What happens next?

Hedda   She drinks.

Hedda *lifts the glass to her mouth.* **Henrik** *does the same.*

Henrik   And he drinks too.

Hedda   And then?

Henrik   She tells him –

Hedda   What?

Henrik   You know what –

Hedda   She tells him the truth.

Hedda *hesitates. She drinks again, then:*

Hedda   The truth is that I might have seemed grown-up – that doesn't mean I was. I lived alone – was working – needed to be close to set. Or far away from anyone who might be looking after me.

Hedda *takes another drink – then continues:*

Hedda   I had – a bottle. Advocaat.

Henrik   You drink that in America?

Hedda   It was a gift. From a producer – male, of course. He'd bought it for me back when we first met – I couldn't have been more than twelve, thirteen. Said he would come back when I was grown-up and we would share it and –

Henrik   And?

Hedda   And – I didn't want that –

Henrik   But you kept the bottle –

Hedda   But I didn't drink it – not until that night. And even then I didn't drink it.

Henrik   No?

Hedda   He did.

Henrik   Ejlert –

Hedda   He didn't smoke – that's true. He asked me for a cigarette – I gave him one. I kissed him – he opened the bottle – drank it all. And I felt – I don't know. Relieved. That it was gone. The prophecy – the older man come back to make his claim – wouldn't come true. Later, we fucked –

Henrik You wanted to?

Hedda I did.

Henrik Did it feel good?

Hedda Does anyone's first time feel good?

Henrik Mine did –

Hedda Does any woman's first time feel good?

Henrik How did you feel then?

Hedda Just – relief. The story wasn't what it might have been.

Henrik It changed –

Hedda It did.

Henrik He changed it –

Hedda No – I did. And I felt – powerful.

Henrik You liked that?

Hedda Doesn't everyone?

Henrik I do – and so do you. I believe you, you know –

Hedda Believe what?

Henrik I don't know what you're capable of.

Hedda I don't know either –

Henrik So – find out.

Thirteen

Jorgen's *trailer. He is drinking, alone.* **Hedda** *enters.*

Hedda Do you have Advocaat?

Jorgen   I have everything.

Hedda *finds the bottle – takes it – then leaves.* **Jorgen** *shouts after her:*

Jorgen   You're welcome!

Hedda *ignores* **Jorgen**, *crossing to her and* **Thea***'s trailer. She enters – finding* **Thea** *and* **Ejlert** *inside, embracing.* **Ejlert** *pulls away from* **Thea**.

Ejlert   This isn't – what it looks like –

Hedda   Oh – you're acting?

Thea   This is – therapy –

Hedda   I'd say it looks more intimate than that –

Thea   I'm also qualified in intimacy co-ordination –

Hedda   I have a scene I need co-ordinated –

Thea   What's the scene?

Hedda   A woman – Hedda – finds out what she's capable of.

Hedda *crosses to* **Ejlert** *– kissing him forcefully.* **Thea** *tries to intervene.*

Thea   Best practice is to state explicitly what will occur within the scene – then gain verbal consent from each participant –

Hedda   I'm going to put my tongue inside his mouth, then let him fuck me any way he wants –

Thea   Okay. And – you consent?

Ejlert   I definitely do.

Thea   Okay, so – please. Proceed.

Ejlert *and* **Hedda** *resume kissing.* **Thea** *steps back – a polite distance.*

Thea   I'll – go. But I'll be – nearby – if you need me.

Thea *continues watching, awkwardly.* **Hedda** *and* **Ejlert** *ignore her.*

Thea   You don't need me, do you? I'll go. I'll – yes – I'll go.

Thea *exits.* **Hedda** *pulls away from* **Ejlert** *– showing him the bottle.*

Ejlert   What's that?

Hedda   You don't recognise it?

Ejlert   Is it – just like –

Hedda   Yes –

Ejlert   It's unopened –

Hedda   Yes. So – open it –

Hedda *hands the bottle to* **Ejlert**. *He hesitates – then opens it.*

Ejlert   What happens next?

Hedda   You drink –

Ejlert   You know that I don't –

Hedda   No – not now. But back then – you remember?

Ejlert   Yes – I do –

Hedda   And don't you want to go back there? To then? To us?

Ejlert   I do –

Hedda   So – drink.

Hedda *takes the bottle, drinks deeply – then kisses* **Ejlert**. *He pulls back – then lifts the bottle to his mouth and drinks.* **Hedda** *turns towards the mirror.*

Hedda   Did you get that, Henrik? Did you? Is that what you want?

Fourteen

Ejlert *and* **Hedda** *in a new space – a balcony, above the set.*
Hedda *is drunk –* **Ejlert** *even more so. He stands at the balcony edge, looking down at the set below – then shuts his eyes and leans over the railing.* **Hedda** *approaches from behind. She pushes him, playfully – then pulls him back.*

Ejlert   Fuck me –

Hedda   Again?

Ejlert   Don't do that – you scared me –

Hedda   Do I?

Ejlert   Scare me? Always did – a little bit –

Hedda   Thank you –

Ejlert   It's not a compliment.

Hedda   What are you doing?

Ejlert   Here? I'm playing Ejlert. And you're Hedda Gabler –

Hedda   Have you read it yet?

Ejlert   I meant to. But I got – distracted –

Hedda   So you don't know how it ends –

Ejlert   Not yet.

Hedda   You die –

Ejlert   I thought I might.

Hedda   How did you know?

Ejlert   First rule of horror movies – you have sex, you die –

Hedda   It's not a horror movie –

Ejlert   Isn't it?

Ejlert *moves to* **Hedda** *and tries to kiss her – but she pulls away.*

Hedda   I meant what you were doing up here –

Ejlert   Just – looking –

Hedda   With your eyes closed?

Ejlert   I was thinking –

Hedda   Thinking? Do you do that?

Ejlert   Don't be cruel. It doesn't suit you.

Hedda   Doesn't it? You know it's my fault – that you die –

Ejlert   You kill me?

Hedda   I put the gun into your hands. I tell you – 'make it beautiful' –

Ejlert   I kill myself?

Hedda   You do.

Ejlert   Fuck. That's –

Hedda   What?

Ejlert   Nothing. I just – should have read the script –

Hedda   There is no script.

A short silence. Again, **Ejlert** *seems drawn towards the balcony's edge.*

Ejlert   It isn't beautiful, you know – it can't be. You said to make it beautiful – but it's not beautiful. I know –

Hedda   How do you know?

Ejlert   I tried. When everything was really bad – I tried. And it – it wasn't beautiful. There was no part of it that could be beautiful.

Hedda   Why did you do that – want to do that –

Ejlert   I guess I felt – trapped. Like I couldn't see another way. You reach a point where everything is so confused that something so grotesque can seem like freedom. Or everything is so grotesque you get confused about what it means to be free.

Hedda   That's what I want –

Ejlert   It isn't – shouldn't be –

Hedda   I don't mean suicide – I mean being free. But I'm like you – I'm trapped. No matter where I go – I'm trapped.

Ejlert   Maybe what's trapping you is you – is inside you –

Hedda   Are you the on-set therapist?

Ejlert   I'm being serious. I mean, like – fear, you know. Or insecurity –

Hedda   Or a baby –

Ejlert   What?

Hedda   I said 'a baby'.

Hedda *hesitates – then laughs.* **Ejlert** *laughs too, unsure.*

Ejlert   I don't get it –

Hedda   I'm not joking.

Ejlert   Then why are you laughing?

Ejlert *laughs again, then lifts the bottle to his mouth – but it is empty.*

Ejlert   We drank all that? Fuck – let's get more –

Ejlert *exits, clumsily.* **Hedda** *remains – looking out over the balcony.*

Hedda   Please – make it beautiful.

Act Three

Fifteen

Hedda *and* **Thea**'s *trailer.* **Hedda** *is vomiting.* **Thea** *enters –*
watching her.

Thea   I have concerns. About you – your drinking –

Hedda   Who says I've been drinking?

Thea   Oh – so it's food poisoning? So how come I'm not
ill –

Hedda   You don't eat food.

Thea   I eat a lot of food –

Hedda   You don't look like it –

Thea   I have a fast metabolism –

Hedda   Lucky you.

Hedda *turns away from* **Thea**, *retching.* **Jorgen** *enters.*

Jorgen   Congratulations! You've shown our movie star for
what he is. A fuck-up, like the rest of us. I heard they found
him passed out in his trailer in a pool of urine –

Hedda   And you're celebrating?

Jorgen   What else is there to celebrate?

Berta *enters. To* **Hedda**, **Thea** *and* **Jorgen**:

Berta   What are you doing here? You're meant to be on
set –

Thea   I'm following up a concern about a colleague, as her
therapist –

Jorgen   And I'm celebrating a concern about a colleague, as
a bitter and competitive man.

Berta   And I'm trying to make a movie. So please – get to set.

Thea *and* **Jorgen** *exit. As* **Hedda** *stands to leave,* **Berta** *stops her.*

Berta   Not you – I want to talk to you –

Hedda   You have concerns about me, too?

Berta   It is my job to have concerns. It's my responsibility to keep you safe – if people are unsafe, they can get hurt – and then my job becomes to clean it up. You stay up drinking, on the set – I clean it up. You fuck each other – fuck each other up – I have to clean it up. You force a man – an addict – to get drunk –

Hedda   I didn't force him –

Berta   Still – I have to clean it up.

Hedda   How do you know about last night –

Berta   My job here is to know. So – tell me –

Hedda   Tell you what?

Berta   If there is anything I need to know.

Hedda *hesitates.* **Berta** *turns to exit – but* **Hedda** *calls after her.*

Hedda   You have a child –

Berta   Yes – a son –

Hedda   And what's he like?

Berta   He's – angry.

Hedda   With you?

Berta   With everything. But yes – with me.

Hedda   And what's it like –

Berta   What – motherhood? Like – giving up –

Hedda   On work?

Berta It's all I do, my work. That's why my son is angry, probably – he wants me for himself. I don't give in – not to that anyway. But all the other things – control. Freedom. To be a parent is to give up almost everything. To – submit.

Hedda To what?

Berta To loving someone else so much you put them first.

Hedda I can't imagine that –

Berta I thought actors can imagine anything.

Hedda What if you can't submit –

Berta You think you can't, but then you do. You think – okay, enough. I've done enough – given enough – there's nothing left. But then – there's more. You think you can't do more – change more, be broken into pieces more – but then you are.

Hedda That sounds horrifying –

Berta It is – but you make it beautiful. Now – get to set. Then I might get to put my kid to bed.

Berta *exits.* **Hedda** *hesitates, then takes out her phone. She makes a call.*

Hedda Hey. It's – me. I know you asked me – told me – not to contact you. I know I really shouldn't contact you. But I just wanted to say – hi. Fuck – I didn't want to say hi. I wanted to – I'm pregnant. And – I know. I know you're busy – with your work, the film, your family. Your real family. But I just wanted to say – that. And to say that – it's cool. I'm cool. I'm a cool girl – who knows better than to ask for more. I'm in Norway, by the way – it sucks. I thought I might find – I don't know. Some kind of peace, out here. Or – change. But – nothing's changed. Has it?

Hedda *hesitates, then hangs up – before immediately checking for a reply. There is none. She puts the phone down by the mirror – then*

shuts her eyes and tries to slow her breathing. **Ejlert** *enters –
hungover, with dried blood across his face.* **Hedda** *opens her eyes
– and jumps.*

Ejlert   I look that bad, do I?

Hedda   You're bleeding –

Ejlert   Probably – I fell off something. This is the part
where you ask what I fell off and I say –

Hedda   You say –

Ejlert   'The wagon.' It's funny –

Hedda   Is it?

Ejlert   You're no fun – not like last night. At least I think
it was fun – I don't remember much. But we should do it
again –

Hedda   No – I don't drink –

Ejlert   You did last night –

Hedda   I shouldn't have –

Ejlert   Why not?

Hedda   I said – last night.

Ejlert   I don't remember –

Hedda   Don't you?

Ejlert   Do you want me to remember?

Hedda   If you do – it makes it real.

Ejlert   So – do you want me to remember?

Hedda's *phone vibrates. She reaches for it – but* **Ejlert** *gets
there first.*

Ejlert   Who is 'Fucking Asshole'? Someone in the industry,
I bet –

Hedda   Give me my phone –

Ejlert   Kiss me.

Hedda   No –

Ejlert   Fuck me, then –

Hedda   No.

Ejlert   Then I won't give you your phone.

Ejlert *holds* **Hedda***'s phone out of reach – then opens the message.*

Ejlert   It says 'Do not ever contact me again'. The message – from the fucking asshole. I mean – they do sound like an asshole –

Hedda   Just – give me back my phone.

Ejlert *gives* **Hedda** *her phone – she throws it at the mirror.*

Ejlert   Are you okay?

Hedda   I'm – no – I'm not –

Ejlert   Come here –

Hedda   I can't – I have to go –

Ejlert   Go where?

Hedda   To work.

Sixteen

On set. **Hedda**, **Thea**, **Berta** *and* **Henrik** *are waiting for* **Ejlert**.

Henrik   Where is he?

Hedda   Who?

Henrik   Your little movie star –

Hedda   How would I know?

Jorgen   Don't play dumb – we all know you and he –

Hedda   There is no me and he – no me and any he. I am
– alone. In Norway, just outside of Oslo, and alone –

Henrik   What happens next?

Hedda   I – die.

Thea   You kill yourself –

Henrik   Not yet – somebody else dies first.

Ejlert *stumbles down the stairs – drunk again – collapsing at*
Henrik*'s feet. He is carrying a bottle of alcohol – he stands,*
unsteadily, then drinks.

Henrik   Okay – he's here. So – we can work.

Berta   Work? But he's drunk –

Henrik   He is. And – in the scene – he's drunk. So –

Berta   It's not safe –

Henrik   I do not care.

Berta   But I have a – responsibility – his welfare –

Henrik   Do you have concerns about his welfare –

Berta   Yes – I –

Henrik   I'm not asking you – I'm asking his therapist.

Thea   Oh – that's me – right, yes – well, I think – as his
therapist – it could be good for him to work. It could be
therapeutic, even –

Henrik   Then let's work. Ejlert –

Ejlert   That's me?

Henrik   That's you. You come in from a night of drinking –

Ejlert   Method acting, baby!

Henrik   To confess to Hedda what you've done –

Ejlert   How long have you got?

Henrik   You tell her that your manuscript is gone. Lost. Thrown away. The work you were most proud of in your life. You've fucked it up. You are fucked up and you have fucked it up. Say it –

Ejlert   I am fucked up and I have fucked it up.

Henrik   You've done the worst thing you could do –

Thea   You've killed a child –

Hedda   What?

Thea   In the original, that's what he says – he's killed a child –

Hedda   Is that the worst thing you can do?

Ejlert   You Europeans have a strange idea of entertainment – child-killing? Suicide?

Jorgen   I'm sorry there is not more police violence and monster trucks –

Ejlert   There's nothing wrong with monster trucks –

Henrik   What happens next?

Hedda   He tells me that he's lost his manuscript – and I don't tell him that it isn't lost. I have it – have his manuscript –

Henrik   What happens next?

Hedda   I burn it –

Ejlert   My manuscript!

Henrik   Why?

Hedda   I – don't know –

Henrik   Don't you? You take his life's work and destroy it –

Hedda   Maybe she – I – just want to destroy – something –

Henrik   Destroy him.

Hedda   No –

Henrik   You do – you do destroy him. Why?

Ejlert   There's no need to destroy me – I'll destroy myself.

Ejlert *drinks*. **Henrik** *turns to* **Berta**.

Henrik   Earpieces, please –

Berta   You want to shoot?

Henrik   No – I want to talk about their feelings. Yes – I want to shoot.

As **Berta** *fetches earpieces for* **Hedda**, **Thea** *and* **Ejlert**, *quietly:*

Berta   Okay, it's just sometimes you do want talk about their feelings –

Hedda   What's this?

Jorgen   An earpiece – so that you don't have to read –

Ejlert   Much appreciated.

Thea   You haven't worked with earpieces before?

Hedda   I assume you have – at the academy –

Thea   He'll give us lines – instructions. And all we have to do –

Henrik   Is everything I say. Are you uncomfortable with that? Say 'no'.

Hedda   No –

Henrik   Very good. You're ready?

Hedda, **Thea** *and* **Berta** *nod*. **Berta** *looks at* **Ejlert**.

Berta   And him – is he ready?

Ejlert   Not yet –

Ejlert *drinks deeply – then wipes his mouth.*

Ejlert   Now I'm ready.

Berta   Rolling. Sound speed. Mark it – action.

Henrik   Ask him what happened –

Thea   What happened, Ejlert?

Henrik   What happened to you?

Thea   What happened to you?

Henrik   To your life's work –

Thea   To your life's work –

Ejlert   I fucked it up.

Berta   Is that the line?

Henrik   That can be the line. You fucked it up –

Ejlert   I fucked it up.

Henrik   You are fucked up –

Ejlert   I am fucked up –

Henrik   And you have fucked it up.

Ejlert   And I have – fucked it up –

Henrik   It's all gone. Lost. Thrown away.

Ejlert   It's all gone – lost – thrown away. Everything I worked for –

Ejlert *starts to cry.* **Thea** *tries to go to him, but* **Henrik** *stops her. To* **Hedda***:*

Henrik   Tell him you're sorry –

Hedda   I am – sorry –

Henrik   Tell him you hate to see him in this state –

Hedda   I do – I hate to see you in this state –

Henrik   But you did this to him –

Hedda   I didn't –

Henrik   Yes – you did.

Ejlert   She didn't. It was me – all me. I did it to myself.

Henrik   She made you drink –

Ejlert   She didn't make me anything. She doesn't have that power.

Henrik   Is that true? That you don't have that power?

Hedda   That's not the kind of power I want –

Henrik   You're sure? I'd rather have that power than have none at all – and be in other people's power, be the one destroyed –

Hedda   You'd rather be the one who causes the destruction?

Henrik   Yes – I would. And I think so would you.

Ejlert   Should I be hearing something through this thing?

Henrik   Tell him –

Hedda   What?

Henrik   That he's wrong – that you have power –

Hedda   I have power –

Henrik   To do what?

Hedda   To – destroy –

Henrik   Destroy what?

Hedda   To destroy – everything.

Ejlert   Seriously – I can't hear a fucking thing –

Henrik   Cut. Good – very good.

Henrik *smiles – then turns to exit.* **Berta** *calls after him:*

Berta   We've finished shooting?

Henrik   We have just begun.

Henrik *exits.* **Berta** *stares after him, confused.*

Berta   I think – we've finished shooting.

Berta *exits –* **Thea** *follows.* **Hedda** *and* **Ejlert** *are alone.*

Ejlert   You think he got my good side?

Hedda   Is that the side with blood on it?

Ejlert *laughs, despite himself – then drains the bottle.*

Ejlert   It's true, isn't it? I'm fucked up and I've fucked it up. The work I was most of proud of in my life is gone. Lost. Thrown away.

Hedda   That isn't true –

Ejlert   Don't lie –

Hedda   I'm acting.

Ejlert   You know what happens next? I finish up the movie – or they make me leave. I call my agent and they fly me home and get me clean. Then I relapse – a year, a month, a moment after that. The same story – again, again, again. I thought if I came out here, then we could change the story – could go back –

Hedda   We did go back –

Ejlert   We did – but I just made the same mistake. I fuck you and I fuck myself. And now I'm here again, with no way to get free –

Hedda   You can get free –

Ejlert   I can't. It's who I am – I can't be anyone but who I am –

Hedda   Come here.

Ejlert *moves to* **Hedda** *– he tries to kiss her, but she stops him, gently. Instead, she undresses him – taking off his shirt, his trousers, socks and shoes. She empties his pockets – takes out his wallet, his ID, a lighter.*

Hedda   You don't smoke.

Ejlert   I quit –

Hedda   But you still have a lighter –

Ejlert   In case I forget I've quit.

Hedda *takes the lighter. She sets alight a piece of paper.*

Ejlert   What's that?

Hedda   A waiver – to say no one can get hurt.

Hedda *uses the paper to set* **Ejlert**'s *belongings alight. As they burn:*

Ejlert   What happens next?

Hedda   You leave. You get free – and we all get free. You're the movie star – without you they can't carry on –

Ejlert   But I don't want to be that anymore – the movie star –

Hedda   And you don't have to be. It's all gone –

Ejlert   Gone – lost – thrown away –

Hedda   You're free –

Ejlert   But I have nothing –

Hedda   Like I said – you're free.

Hedda *opens a door. For the first time, the world outside appears – ice and snow and concrete, harsh and unforgiving.* **Ejlert** *stares at it in disbelief.*

Hedda   Here – take this –

Hedda *holds out her hand to* **Ejlert** *– in it is the 1,000 kroner note.*

Hedda   A thousand kroner note – enough to get a taxi to the airport –

Ejlert   And go where?

Hedda   Go anywhere.

Ejlert   You're joking?

Hedda   Hedda Gabler's not a comedy.

Ejlert   I wouldn't know – I never read it –

Hedda   Here –

Again, **Hedda** *holds out her hand – in it is a copy of Hedda Gabler.*

Ejlert   But I already know the ending –

Hedda   So do I.

Ejlert *takes the book – then turns and steps towards the door.*
Hedda *watches him leave – then shuts the door behind him and turns back to the fire. As she watches it, transfixed,* **Henrik**'s *voice is heard in her ear.*

Henrik   Keep going, Hedda –

Hedda   Hedda's not my name –

Henrik   It can be – if you keep going –

Hedda *takes a breath – then steps towards the flames.*

Hedda   I just –

Henrik   What?

Hedda   Just want to be free.

Hedda *steps into the flames. They rise around her – and she disappears.*

Act Four

Seventeen

Hedda *is collapsed.* **Berta** *wakes her, helps her into a shower – then exits.* **Henrik** *enters – waits for* **Hedda**. *She leaves the shower.*

Henrik   Where is he?

Hedda   Who?

Henrik   You know who – Ejlert –

Hedda   I – don't know –

Henrik   You're sure?

Hedda   Why would I know?

Berta *enters. She tries to cross the stage, but* **Henrik** *stops her.*

Hedda   He's late –

Berta   I know – I'll check his trailer –

Henrik   So are you. We were supposed to start at ten –

Berta   I know – but I'm –

Henrik   I need you here. We need to shoot.

Berta   But we can't shoot – he isn't here –

Henrik   So we'll shoot something else. The gun –

Berta   You need the gun?

Henrik How can she shoot herself, if we don't have the gun?

Berta   And Ejlert –

Henrik   If he comes, he comes – if not, I'll find somebody else. You like to think you're not replaceable – you are. Now get the gun.

Over the following, **Berta** *exits – returning with the gun.*

Hedda   You want to shoot –

Henrik   Your suicide. You're ready?

Hedda   For my suicide?

Henrik   Or are you still afraid?

Hedda   I never said I was afraid –

Henrik   You didn't have to.

Berta *hands the gun to* **Henrik**. *He holds it out to* **Hedda** *– she takes it.*

Henrik   In your hand is a gun. It's heavy – real. Maybe the gun is – in the end – the only thing that's real. Just Hedda – and the gun.

Hedda   What happens next?

Henrik   You know what happens next.

Hedda   I – shoot –

Henrik   The only action left for you to take. So – shoot.

Hedda *hesitates – then lifts the gun. She aims it at herself.*

Hedda   Like this?

Henrik   Like that.

Hedda *shuts her eyes – places her finger on the trigger.*

Berta   Wait –

Hedda *opens her eyes.* **Berta** *holds out gloves and safety goggles.*

Berta   So you don't get hurt.

Hedda   It – hurts?

Henrik   It's suicide. You think it doesn't hurt?

Hedda *puts on the safety equipment – then lifts the gun again.*

Henrik You look –

Hedda   What?

Henrik Beautiful. It suits you.

Hedda   Fuck you.

Hedda *pulls the trigger. A gunshot. She falls.* **Henrik** *shakes his head.*

Henrik   No. I don't believe it.

Berta   Blood?

Henrik   Let's try the blood.

As **Hedda** *gets to her feet,* **Berta** *affixes a blood pack to her chest.*

Berta   Again?

Henrik   Again.

Hedda   But – I already did it –

Henrik   Did you? Kill yourself? So why are you still here?

Hedda   I don't know –

Henrik   Yes – you do. Again.

Hedda   I can't –

Henrik   You can. Again.

Hedda   How many times?

Henrik   Until I can believe your pain –

Hedda   I am – in pain –

Henrik   I don't believe you –

Hedda   But I am.

Henrik   Again –

Berta   You want to go again?

Henrik   I want to see this pain.

Again **Hedda** *lifts the gun. She pulls the trigger. A gunshot. She falls. As she stands – more slowly this time – a bloodstain spreads across her chest.*

Henrik   I still don't – no –

Berta   You need more blood?

Henrik   It's not the blood – it isn't real –

Berta   It – isn't real –

Henrik   Why not?

Berta   Because – it can't be. It's – a suicide. It can't be real –

Henrik   Why not? Why fucking not? *Why can't you give me what I want? You cannot even understand – imagine – what I want. Instead you're always looking at your watch, asking me when you get to eat or smoke or leave. It is a privilege, you know, to starve to make this work. You understand? A privilege –*

Hedda   I don't understand –

Berta   He is – concerned –

Hedda   About me?

Berta   No – about the scene –

Henrik   Yes – about you – in the scene. Now – go again.

Hedda   Again?

Henrik   We go again – until you give me what I want, Hedda –

Hedda   That's not my name –

Henrik   That is your name, Hedda! Again!

Hedda   I – can't –

Henrik   Then give me something else.

Hedda   What do you want –

Henrik   The truth, Hedda – I want the truth.

Hedda   The truth is that – I'm trapped. In Norway, in a house with thick stone walls. Or on a movie set. Or in a small town by the interstate – a house that never properly gets dark. In every place, the story ends the same – again, again, again – with no way to escape. No matter where I go – how many times I leave – I end up trapped. There is no other ending – only failure, madness – suicide. I drive my car into a stranger with a camera – another stranger takes a photo of me passed out on the floor. They take a photo as I leave the car with bruises – take a photo when my father dies. They take a photo through the window – of the bathroom, of the dressing room, the hospital. There is no place they will not take a photo. I thought if I came here –

Henrik   You thought there'd be no cameras? On a film set?

Hedda   I didn't think. I only wanted –

Henrik   What?

Hedda   To get – away. To find some kind of change. To change. But now I understand – you cannot change. You cannot get away. No matter where you go, some things – they follow you. You follow you. I can't be anyone but who I am. And so –

Henrik   What happens next?

As **Hedda** *slowly lifts the gun:*

Hedda   In my hand is a gun. It's heavy – real – maybe the only thing that is. The world around me feels unreal. I feel unreal – have felt unreal for such a long, long time. I lift the gun. I aim it at myself. I shoot –

Before **Hedda** *can pull the trigger, there is the sound of a champagne cork popping –* **Jorgen** *and* **Thea** *enter with a bottle and glasses, celebrating.*

> **Thea**   *Congratulations!*

Hedda   What's this?

Jorgen   You haven't heard?

Thea   They've just announced – you have been nominated!

Hedda   Nominated? For what?

Jorgen   Not you – him –

Henrik   Me?

Thea   Of course! And rightly so!

Henrik   Please – I don't do this work to win awards –

Jorgen   Not even the most prestigious cinema award in Europe?

Thea   Europe? In the world!

Jorgen   To the best director in the motherfucking world!

As **Jorgen** *toasts* **Henrik,** **Hedda** *touches her chest. She is bleeding.*

Hedda   I'm bleeding –

Berta   No – you're not. It's from a blood pack –

Jorgen   How does it feel?

Hedda   It feels – real –

Jorgen   I'm not talking to you –

Henrik   It feels – unreal. Although – it's just a nomination –

Jorgen   Soon-to-be award!

Henrik   And it's not just acknowledgement of me – but all of you. Your willingness to place your lives into my hands – I'll drink to that.

Jorgen *and* **Thea** *raise their glasses, toasting* **Henrik.** *To* **Hedda***:*

Thea   You're not drinking?

Hedda   I'm not in the mood –

Thea   Because you are depressed? Experiencing a mid-life crisis?

Hedda   Because – I'm bleeding –

Berta   It's not real –

Thea   It looks real. Henrik, you've outdone yourself –

Henrik   It isn't me – it's her. She makes it real. Show them.

Hedda   Show them?

Henrik   The way you make it real.

Hedda *lifts the gun and pulls the trigger. A gunshot. She falls – harder this time. As she stands – now visibly in pain –* **Thea** *applauds.*

Thea   Bravo! Again!

Hedda   Again?

Jorgen   Again!

Henrik   You heard them – go again.

Hedda *begins to lift the gun – but* **Berta** *stops her.*

Berta   You're going to hurt her –

Henrik   And?

Berta   And it won't be pretend. It will be real –

Henrik   That's what I want.

Berta   You're going to really hurt her –

Henrik   No. I only want to see how far it goes –

Hedda   You know how far it goes. I die –

Berta   You don't die – Hedda does. It's different –

Hedda   But it feels the same.

Henrik   Again.

As **Hedda** *puts her finger on the trigger, a phone rings.* **Henrik** *answers.*

Henrik   *Hello? Yes – speaking. Who is this?*

Jorgen   It's the awards committee –

Thea   Calling to say that he has won –

Jorgen   Of course he's won! I'll get some more champagne –

Berta   We're working –

Jorgen   With the best director in the motherfucking world!

Thea *and* **Jorgen** *whoop.* **Henrik** *turns to them, sharply.*

Henrik   *Quiet!*

Hedda, Berta, Thea *and* **Jorgen** *listen, as* **Henrik** *speaks to the caller.*

Henrik   *They found him? Where? And when was this? And he is – yes. You're sure? That's – yes, a shock. I understand. And – what?*

Henrik *turns to stare at* **Hedda,** *as he listens. She shifts, uncomfortable.*

Henrik   *Thank you – that's very helpful. Yes – I know that name. Okay.*

Henrik *hangs up. He turns to* **Berta.**

Henrik   That was security. They just completed a patrol. They found him – Ejlert –

Berta   In his trailer?

Henrik   No. There's been a – medical emergency – outside –

Berta   I'll go. I'll go now. Can I go?

Henrik   Yes – go.

Berta *exits.*

Thea   He's ill?

Jorgen   It's serious?

Henrik   I don't know any more than you. Now please –
we're working.

Thea   Yes – of course –

Thea *and* **Jorgen** *start to exit.* **Jorgen** *is still drinking his champagne.*

Thea   Don't!

Jorgen   What?

Thea   Don't drink champagne – it could be serious –

Jorgen   And? That means I can't drink champagne?

Jorgen *and* **Thea** *exit.* **Hedda** *and* **Henrik** *are alone. She is shaking.*

Henrik   Where were we? Yes – your suicide –

Hedda   What's happening?

Henrik   We're getting ready for your suicide –

Hedda   What did they say?

Henrik   Who?

Hedda   On the phone – what happened –

Henrik   Don't you know?

Hedda   I – don't –

Henrik   I don't believe you.

Hedda   Tell me, please –

Henrik   You want to know? They found his body –

Hedda   Body?

Henrik   In the snow –

Hedda   They found his – body –

Henrik   He was barefoot – in underwear. He froze to
death –

Hedda   To death? He's dead? I have to go – to see him –

Henrik   I don't think you do. Believe me – when a body comes in contact with a snowplough –

Hedda   A snowplough?

Henrik   It's heavy machinery –

Hedda   I thought he froze –

Henrik   He did. And then the snowplough –

Hedda *turns away.* **Henrik** *watches her – then starts to clap.*

Henrik   Very good – very convincing –

Hedda   What?

Henrik   Whatever else they say about you – you can act.

Hedda   I'm – not acting –

Henrik   No?

Hedda   I'm – in shock –

Henrik   Are you sure? You didn't know?

Hedda   That he was dead? Of course not –

Henrik   But you knew that he was out there, in the snow –

Hedda   No – I –

Henrik   Don't lie.

Hedda   I'm not –

Henrik   They told me he was almost naked – stripped of his belongings – all except –

Hedda   Except –

Henrik   One thousand kroner – and a book. Hedda Gabler. Your copy. Your name, written on the inside cover – like a child. Not surprising – for a child actor –

Hedda   No –

Henrik   Your name, found on the body of a dead man. A man who came here in a fragile state. You gave him alcohol – encouraged him to drink. You made him relapse and then sent him out into the snow. Into the night. To die.

Hedda   I didn't mean –

Henrik   You did, Hedda.

Hedda   That's not my name –

Henrik   It can be –

Hedda   I don't want that – no – I don't want any of this –

Henrik   But you do. You did this. All of this was you.

Hedda   How do you know?

Henrik   It is my job – to see the truth.

Hedda   That's not the truth –

Henrik   It is.

Hedda: What happens next –

Henrik   A man is dead. Police will be involved. Prisons in Norway are extremely comfortable – but I don't think you'd like it there.

Hedda   You'll tell them –

Henrik   Yes. Unless –

Hedda   You want something –

Henrik   I do.

Hedda   What do you want?

Henrik   The truth. You give me truth and I will lie for you – I'll say you weren't with him last night. And everything that happened – getting drunk and walking off into the night – he did it all himself. An act of self-destruction. Suicide.

Hedda   And I –

Henrik   Were with somebody else. With me. Of course, they'd ask me questions, ask for details – about you – your body –

Hedda   What about my body?

Henrik   I just want to know the truth.

Henrik *approaches* **Hedda**. *She shuts her eyes – but stands her ground.*

Hedda   And – what about the book –

Henrik   It disappears.

Hedda   If you do that –

Henrik   What do you do for me?

Henrik *reaches out to touch* **Hedda**. *She tenses.*

Hedda   What – do you – want –

Henrik   I told you – just the truth.

Henrik *undoes* **Hedda**'s *clothing – revealing her pregnancy. He stares at her.*

Henrik   You're her. You're really her. How many weeks?

Hedda   I – don't know –

Henrik   Yes – you do.

Hedda   Seventeen –

Henrik   What will you do?

Hedda   I – don't know –

Henrik   Yes – you do. But first – we have to work.

Henrik *turns away from* **Hedda**. **Berta** *enters.*

Berta   Henrik – you heard?

Henrik   I did –

Berta   I can't believe it – I'm in shock –

Henrik   Where are the others?

Berta   They're – in shock –

Henrik   They're meant to be on set. We have to work.

Berta   What work?

Henrik   The film –

Berta   You want to carry on?

Henrik   Why not?

Berta   A man is dead –

Henrik   And? Does that mean the film is complete?

Berta   But there are more important things –

Henrik   There are not more important things!

Berta   A man – is dead –

Henrik   You said –

Berta   And we need – time to grieve –

Henrik   We have the on-set therapist –

Berta   And she needs time to grieve!

Thea *and* **Jorgen** *enter.* **Henrik** *turns to* **Thea***.*

Henrik   Do you need time to grieve? Or can you carry on?

Thea   I – I can carry on –

Henrik   And you?

Jorgen   Of course – although, if I may ask – now Ejlert has departed – sadly – could I throw my hat into the ring? As a mark of respect, of course – as an homage –

Henrik   There is no need for your homage.

Berta   You've found someone? To take his place?

Henrik   I told you – none of you is irreplaceable.

Ejlert *enters. When he speaks, it is in a Norwegian accent. To* **Hedda***:*

Ejlert   Hi – great to meet you – I am such a fan –

Hedda   I'm sorry – I don't understand –

Ejlert   Of you – your work – I love the movie where you went to prom –

Hedda   You're – him –

Ejlert   That's kind – that's really kind. A lot of people say I look like him – so obviously, in the circumstances, it makes sense –

Hedda   You really look like him –

Ejlert   It's lucky – I mean, not for him – not lucky that he's dead –

Hedda   What the fuck is going on –

Ejlert   She knows, right? That he's dead?

Hedda   This isn't – you aren't real – this can't be real –

Henrik   It is. That is –

Hedda   What is –

Henrik   The gun.

Hedda *notices the gun in her hand. She seems surprised – repulsed – by it.*

Hedda   No – I don't want a gun –

Henrik   You need a gun. You give it to him –

Hedda   No – I don't –

Henrik   He is your lover – oldest friend. He is – undone. By drink, by fire – and by you. He comes to ask you for your help. But you don't help him – do you? Do you help him, Hedda?

Hedda   I – I try –

Henrik   You don't. You put the gun into his hands –

Hedda   I didn't – no –

Henrik   You tell him – 'make it beautiful' –

Hedda   It can't be beautiful –

Henrik   You send him to his death –

Hedda: I don't – I won't –

Henrik   You do, Hedda. You know you do.

Hedda   I can't –

Henrik   You will. You do. You already have.

Berta *brings on earpieces. As she fits* **Hedda***'s,* **Hedda** *pleads with her.*

Hedda   Please – help me, please –

Berta *hesitates – then turns away.* **Henrik** *leans close to* **Hedda***.*

Henrik   The only thing you have to do is everything I say.

Berta   Rolling. Sound speed. Mark it – action.

Henrik   I heard you had a quite exciting night.

Hedda   I – heard you – had a – quite – exciting night –

Henrik   It was exciting – rather too exciting, actually.

Ejlert   It was exciting – rather too exciting, actually.

Henrik   Things got – quite out of hand.

Ejlert   Things got – quite out of hand.

Henrik   By daybreak, everything was utterly destroyed.

Hedda   By daybreak – everything was – utterly destroyed –

Henrik   That's his line – not yours –

Ejlert   By daybreak, everything was utterly destroyed.

Hedda   Destroyed –

Henrik   That's his line –

Hedda   I'm sorry – no – I can't –

Henrik   You do not say 'I can't', you say 'like what'?

Hedda   Like what?

Henrik   Like me. My life. All gone. Lost. Thrown away.

Ejlert   Like me. My life –

Hedda   It's not my fault –

Henrik   That's not the line –

Hedda   I only wanted for you to be free – for us to both be free –

Henrik   That isn't – no – that's not the line –

Hedda   But I can see now that it isn't possible –

Henrik   The line is 'here' –

Hedda   Not here – not anywhere –

Henrik   You put the gun into his hand – you tell him 'make it beautiful' –

Hedda   It isn't – can't be – beautiful – it can't –

Hedda *sinks to the floor, still holding the gun.*

Berta   You're going to kill her –

Henrik   No – she isn't capable of that.

Hedda   You don't know what I'm capable of –

Henrik   I do. And I see now that I was wrong – you're not her. So –

Jorgen   You need somebody to play Hedda? I know I'm not the obvious choice, but –

Henrik   No. I want the other one –

Berta   The other one?

Henrik   We have two, don't we? So – I want the other one –

Thea   That's me? The other one? What do you need – from me –

Henrik   Just say the line – it's finished –

Thea   Okay – I –

Henrik   Just say the line!

Over the following, **Hedda** *staggers to her feet – still holding the gun.*

Thea   It's finished –

Henrik   It's time –

Thea   It's time –

Henrik   For what?

Ejlert   For what?

Henrik   You know what.

Thea   You know what.

Henrik   Just make it beautiful.

Thea   Just make it –

Hedda   No. It won't be – can't be – beautiful. Whatever happens next – it won't be beautiful. It will be ugly, painful, violent – the end of everything. No – that's too poetic. And it won't be poetic –

Henrik   Fuck! Get her out of here – I'm done with her – I'm finished –

Hedda   It's all finished. So – it's time. Just – make it beautiful –

Berta *crosses to* **Hedda** *– but* **Hedda** *moves away, towards the exit.*

Henrik   Go again. By daybreak, everything was utterly destroyed –

Ejlert   By daybreak, everything was utterly destroyed –

Henrik   Like what?

Thea   Like what?

Hedda   Like me. My life. All gone. Lost. Thrown away –

Hedda *exits, with the gun – almost unnoticed.*

Henrik   Again! Go again –

Ejlert   By daybreak, everything was totally destroyed –

Henrik   Utterly –

Ejlert   Was utterly destroyed – by daybreak –

Jorgen   Could I try –

Ejlert   Everything was utterly destroyed –

Jorgen   By daylight, everything was utterly destroyed –

Thea   Daybreak, daybreak –

Henrik   By daybreak, everything was utterly destroyed!

A gunshot. **Henrik, Berta, Thea, Ejlert** *and* **Jorgen** *turn, as* **Hedda**'s *body is revealed in her trailer. A moment of stillness – then chaos, as* **Berta, Thea** *and* **Jorgen** *rush to* **Hedda. Henrik** *remains frozen, staring.*

Henrik   You did it. Oh, Hedda – you stupid girl. You really did it.

Henrik *steps backward – shocked – then exits. Only* **Ejlert** *is left on set.*

Ejlert   Should I – go again?

Printed in the USA
CPSIA information can be obtained
at www.ICGtesting.com
LVHW020856171024
794056LV00002B/572